DIGITAL CAREER BUILDING™

CAREER BUILDING THROUGH

SOCIAL NETWORKING

ALEX GOETCHIUS

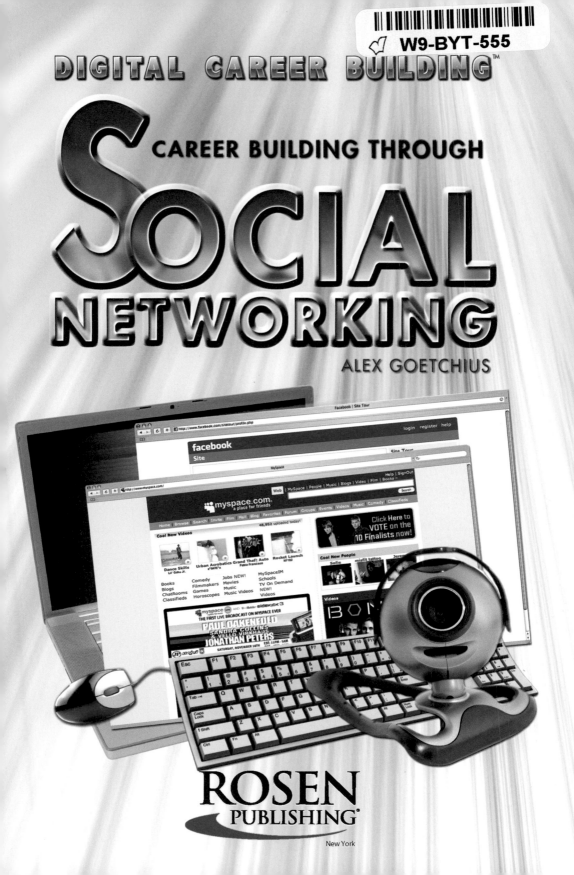

ROSEN
PUBLISHING®

New York

For Lukas

Published in 2008 by The Rosen Publishing Group, Inc.
29 East 21st Street, New York, NY 10010

Copyright © 2008 by The Rosen Publishing Group, Inc.

First Edition

Library of Congress Cataloging-in-Publication Data

Goetchius, Alex.
Career building through social networking / Alex Goetchius.
     p. cm. — (Digital career building)
Includes bibliographical references and index.
ISBN-13: 978-1-4042-1943-4
ISBN-10: 1-4042-1943-9
1. Social networks. 2. Career development. I. Title.
HM131.G5354 2008
650.1'3—dc22

                                                        2007001624

Manufactured in the United States of America

CONTENTS

CHAPTER ONE

SOCIAL NETWORKING COMES INTO ITS OWN

Today, people live online. They shop, play, and work online. People buy products from virtual stores, and they build relationships with others they've never met in person. Using the computer to "travel" the Internet is like moving from place to place in a time machine. Every stop along the way is filled with people and places that you'd otherwise never know, and each person and place will inspire you in a new and different way. The Internet has become a great means for people to find others who share their opinions. Through these connections, they may exchange ideas.

Today, the Internet has also become a launching pad for careers in new industries. You probably know

More and more, people all over the world are using social networks to gain exposure for their creative projects and business ventures.

that the Internet is a virtual doorway to instant information about current events and facts, as well as a path into an endless stream of music, video, and film. But did you know you could use the Internet to launch your career? By offering online information about yourself and what you do, you can reach thousands of people who might be interested in who you are, what you have done, and what you have to say.

In addition to creating a personal Web site, which may be too costly to produce, or too complicated or time-consuming to update, the most popular use of the Internet as a tool to express yourself is through the use of social networks. These virtual communities help connect people and allow them to express themselves. Usually, members of these communities have some things in common.

Changing the Way We Communicate

Interacting within the confines of a social network is a primary way that people communicate. Social networks also make conversing with large groups of people easy and effective. These networks are largely made up of people who create a virtual identity, usually in the form of a personal profile, as is the case with networks such as MySpace, Facebook, and Friendster. Profile pages utilize Internet applications and tools, including e-mail, instant messaging (IMing), group chats, groups, forums, blogs, and vlogs. Social networking evolved into a way to create a more complete virtual existence by combining text and images about yourself or about how you see the world. These profile

pages are similar to Web pages, which can have personal or professional functions. The interconnection of these profiles is what makes up a social network, or online community.

Social networks have been in use on the Internet since 1995. The first social network, which is still in existence today was Classmates.com. This network is made up of alumni from U.S. high schools and colleges who can register on the site to offer information about their current whereabouts. People register on Classmates.com, offer the name of the high school or college where they graduated from and their graduating year, and use this information to connect them with other members of their graduating class. Classmates.com currently has more than forty million registered users.

The Internet has given the average person the ability to communicate with thousands or even tens of thousands of people at one time. Today, online communities are small towns filled with hundreds of thousands of businesses and millions of people.

Marketing and Advertising

Social networks allow you to find and connect with specific people from all over the world who share your interests and ideas. MySpace and Facebook, for example, are no longer a secondary means of marketing and promotion. They have become a main tool and have proven their worth in getting businesses and products name recognition. One example of social networking used as a marketing tool is the case of the motion-picture industry.

On this MySpace page (MySpace.com), actor Will Ferrell portrays Ron Burgundy, a character in the film *Anchorman: The Legend of Ron Burgundy*. Even major motion-picture companies use social networks for promotion.

Most major motion-picture companies are bypassing the idea of establishing their own Web sites and are using MySpace profiles as their primary promotional vehicles. Some industry marketers are even creating fictional profiles on such sites to promote their companies' films, as was the case with DreamWorks' character Ron Burgundy, played by Will Ferrell in *Anchorman: The Legend of Ron Burgundy* (2004), and Universal's Jason Bourne, played by Matt Damon in *The Bourne Supremacy* (2004).

Businesses such as Proctor & Gamble were early users of marketing via social networks, as seen in that company's 2004 launch of a deodorant called Secret Sparkle, a sister product of the popular Secret brand for

women. Proctor & Gamble used profile pages of popular teen actresses to endorse the new deodorant, and then it asked teens to enter a contest that required them to join a mailing list maintained by the company. In this case, as in many others, businesses are finding it easier to attract potential customers to their social network pages than their own dedicated Web site. In 2007, companies such as JPMorgan Chase, Volkswagon, and American Eagle Outfitters were all tapping into the popularity and unique marketing opportunities now available on social networks.

Along with MySpace, which is the most popular online community with more than 140 million members, there are literally hundreds of social networks, each catering to different needs. The following are just a few of the most popular social networks:

- **MySpace** MySpace was bought by News Corp. in 2005 for $580 million and has since become the leading social network. It was started for musicians as a showcase for their music. It now offers users the ability to share audio and video files, animation, writing, photographs, and illustrations. In 2006, MySpace went global, offering services in at least ten European countries.
- **Friendster** Friendster was one of the first social networks and was awarded the patent for social networking in June 2006. Friendster was considered the most popular social network until 2004, when MySpace overshadowed it. In 2006, Friendster had about thirty million members.

Just as like-minded students form cliques, the social networking site Tribe.net allows members to form "tribes" to discuss anything from popular celebrities to politics.

- **Tribe** Tribe features so-called tribes as topical forums. Any user can create a forum. When a user creates a new tribe, he or she becomes the official moderator of that tribe. Any user can join any tribe. Tribes are similar to forums of like-minded users and can house photos, news articles, and information about local events and more.

- **Facebook** A social networking site that started at Harvard University, Facebook now boasts more than eight million student profiles that make up its ten million unique users. In the fall of 2006, Facebook launched a feature called NewsFeed, which allows users to keep up with the activities of other people within the network.

Flickr (Flickr.com), the popular photo-sharing network, contains millions of photos that are searchable to members and nonmembers. Increasingly, professional print publishers are using amateur work directly from the Internet.

- **Flickr** This site is primarily visual in that it allows users to upload photographs or images of artwork, making the works viewable to other members who can comment on them, collect them, and add them to specific groups.
- **hi5** Hi5 is an online service that has a set of unique features, such as enabling users to purchase songs via iTunes to add to their profile. Hi5 has more than 50 million members.
- **FriendFinder** FriendFinder is a global online relationship network with more than 25 million members.
- **FriendSurfer** FriendSurfer is a six-degrees-of-separation online experiment. Six degrees of separation

If you think that your taste in music rocks, you can join hi5 (hi5.com), a social network that lets users rate songs and feature their MP3 files, courtesy of Apple's iTunes software.

is a theory that suggests every person in the world is connected to one another through just six other people. In other words, you are connected to your friends, your friends' friends, your friends' friends' friends, and so on. Your friends' matrix is made up of the people with whom you are directly (or indirectly) connected.

- **Yahoo! 360** Yahoo! 360 is Yahoo!'s social networking site, which brings together blogging and photosharing.
- **TagWorld** TagWorld has a music discovery engine and an IM client with video chat. It boasts a notable feature that allows users to upload one gigabyte of music, pictures, and video to the site for later

TagWorld (TagWorld.com) allows members to create profiles filled with multi-media content, including video, photography, music, and instant communication via IMing and video chat.

playback from anywhere with an Internet connection. In January 2007, TagWorld had nearly two million members.

- **Gaia** Gaia is for those who enjoy anime and computer gaming. Users of the site, known as Gaians, create avatars that they can purchase by using "gaia gold," which they receive for interacting on the site. Gaians number about five million.

- **GreatestJournal** GreatestJournal is a community of bloggers who keep daily journals online. This site also offers video hosting, voice posts, and image galleries. GreatestJournal has nearly two million members.

GreatestJournal (GreatestJournal.com) permits users to create a modern diary complete with video and audio components. Imagine how your daily entries can come alive with multimedia content.

- **Craigslist** This social networking site, which focuses users geographically, combines the idea of classified advertising and social networking. Craigslist is like a vast community bulletin board that a person can use to find a job, used furnishings, concert tickets, a dogwalker, a Web designer, or someone to teach him or her tai chi. No matter what a person is looking for, it can be found on Craigslist.
- **Panjéa** Panjéa combines social networking with e-commerce. It enables artists to earn money in several ways.
- **Cyworld** Cyworld was first started in South Korea in 1999 and had daily revenues averaging up to $300,000

Panjéa is among the social networks that allow members to earn money from their content. In addition to direct sales of handmade items, members are compensated based on the popularity of their pages.

in September 2005. It has since become a large community in the United States. Its primary feature is a service called a minihompy, which combines a user profile, photo gallery, message board, guest book, video, and personal bulletin board. Cyworld members use money called *dotori*, which is translated as "acorns." Users can link with one another's minihompy and embellish their minihompies with fonts, wallpapers, and other decorations.

- **Tagged** Tagged, a teen social networking site that was founded in 2004, contains the unique concept of being "tagged," building "tag teams," and earning points to become the "Ultimate Tagged Team."

Tagged (Tagged.com) is a site geared specifically to teens. Like MySpace, Tagged relies on user profiles as its main attraction.

- **Popist** Popist is similar to MySpace but has more open features, such as enabling users to integrate with other social networks.

Vast Career Possibilities

The digital skills that are commonly used for navigating and participating in social networks also can be applied to future careers. Writers, animators, filmmakers, musicians, graphic designers, bloggers, and gamers can utilize the digital skills they've developed when seeking professional jobs. If you are able to move your work from the analog world to the digital world, you may find a larger selection of careers from which to choose. If you

Popist (Popist.com) has become a popular social network for teens because it lets users rate their content against profile pages on other sites. Using Popist, you can find friends on many different sites and link them back to your profile.

have a talent for drawing pictures, editing photographs, or creating Web content, a career in graphic design may be of interest to you. If you are a musician and have become skilled in using the computer to create and record music, there is an abundance of work for composers and audio engineers in the digital world. If you have dabbled in creating your videos by using a camcorder and a computer to edit the footage, then you might consider a career in filmmaking. Musicians interested in soundtrack work and audio editing are applying their skills to Internet businesses that concern audio content. Filmmakers are finding work creating commercials and video content for Web sites. It's also easier to find work when using social networks because artists' portfolios and résumés are now reaching millions of people, rather than mere hundreds.

This book describes how social networking can be used effectively to turn a hobby or an idea into a career—largely related to the arts. However, the same principles can be applied to any interest, from athletics and modeling to science and food, to help you in your search for a rewarding profession.

CHAPTER TWO

CONNECTING TO THE MASSES

People who once thought that only a select group could carve out a career from their hobbies can now see people creating livelihoods merely by marketing a concept. The Internet has improved people's chances at establishing careers in new and exciting ways and enabled them to try out aspects of a career choice before fully committing themselves to it.

Before the widespread use of social networks, artists, musicians, writers, performers, photographers, and video and filmmakers had to spread their message by hitting the pavement. In the past, artists have used traditional tools for communicating, such as postal mail and the telephone, to get their work seen by a greater

In addition to being a vast warehouse of information, the Internet is also a place to make contacts, get feedback, and build careers.

variety of people. Today, when using social networks, hundreds of thousands of people around the world can be reached as easily as clicking a mouse. As a result of reaching such a large number of people, artists are finally able to get their work into the hands of gallery owners, critics, collaborators, journalists, publishers, investors, producers, consumers, and any others who may be able to help launch their careers.

Branding Your Ideas

Other people are using online networks to brand their ideas in a single catchphrase, plastering it over T-shirts and hats, bumper stickers and decals, surfboards and skateboards, and sneakers and toys. They have tapped into a vein rich with potential by marketing themselves as a unique entity to the millions who are connected to the Internet. One such example is Life Is Good, which was founded in 1994 and sells optimism. Life Is Good is an $80 million-a-year company born from the simple idea and slogan, "Life is good." Brothers Bert and John Jacobs created their trademark character, Jake, a stick figure enjoying outdoor activities such as skiing, surfing, and canoeing.Over the next decade, the Jacobs brothers have used that slogan and Jake on more than 900 items from dog bowls to furniture. Life Is Good searches all over the Internet lead back to Bert and John Jacobs. They've done a masterful job of getting their message to college and high school students, who make up the largest percentage of the Web population and who can be found on any number of social networks.

The Internet has made the unlikely completely possible. For instance, just a decade ago, few people would have believed that a Web site such as Life Is Good (LifeIsGood.com) could sell hundreds of products with a logo.

Gaining Exposure

Musicians have often run into dead ends when trying to get their music heard and distributed, and have found gathering a following through live performances a very slow go. Record labels are a tight-knit society, and many don't have the time, manpower, or interest to listen to every band that comes for an audition, and they are less willing to devote dollars to unproven acts. Even independent record labels have gained success through their Internet presence over the last decade, making it possible for lesser-known bands to get increased exposure.

With social networks such as MySpace, however, bands can bypass the major labels. Those who have the skill and desire to utilize the tools that social networks offer can promote and distribute their music themselves, retaining the copyright to their songs and selling their CDs independently through Web sites such as CD Baby. This venue gives the bands total control of their product and image, and in some cases enables them to reach just as many people as the gigantic marketing machines employed by conventional record labels.

 The Arctic Monkeys (www.arcticmonkeys. com), a four-piece post-punk band from England, bypassed the entire process of shopping their material to major labels and instead achieved success in 2003 through fan-shared demo tapes and Internet file-sharing. The band handed out demo tapes to their friends at gigs, the tapes were copied and uploaded onto the Internet, and the band's music spread across the Web like wildfire. Multiple Arctic Monkey profiles popped up on sites such as MySpace. Soon after, the band performed live shows to crowds who would sing along, word for word, to songs that had never been commercially released. Eventually, the Arctic Monkeys signed with Domino Records, an independent label, and in January 2006 they released their first album, *Whatever People Say I Am, That's What I'm Not*. It debuted at the number-one spot and broke all records for sales of a debut album in the United Kingdom in 2006.

Writers have also had to contend with various industry roadblocks and obstacles on their quest to be on best-seller lists. Often writers find that the distribution for their books is hard to come by, and audiences at their book readings are sometimes limited to a handful of friends. Consequently, some writers have taken to creating Internet blogs, which are similar to Web sites and act as daily journals. Some blogs provide news and commentary, while others serve as online diaries. Blogs can contain words and images, as well as links to other blogs, Web sites, or audio and video clips. Many blogs offer "slice of life" pieces or writing in a stream-of-consciousness style. And although many blog readers are family and friends of the writers, more and more bloggers are gaining widespread success as blogs are transformed into newspaper and magazine articles and, in some cases, books. Stephanie Klein took this untraditional path to success. Her first novel, *Straight Up and Dirty*, is based on her well-read blog, Geek Tragedy. Another blog-writer-turned-book-author is the

Since the blogging trend began in the late 1990s, Web sites such as Technorati (technorati.com) have been keeping track of the blogging community by mapping what is hot and what is not.

anonymous Riverbend, whose blog about life in Baghdad, Iraq, under the U.S. occupation became highly popular in 2005.

There are literally millions of blogs. According to Technorati (www.technorati.com, a Web site that monitors blogs), about 100,000 new blogs are created each day. Some of the more popular ones are about art, such as Drawn! (Drawn.ca) and We Make Money Not Art (www.we-make-money-not-art.com). There are also media and culture blogs, such as Boing Boing (www.boingboing.net) and Fark (www.fark.com).

Filmmakers face the same problems that musicians and writers do in gaining exposure to their work. Often

Boing Boing (BoingBoing.com) is among America's most widely read blogs. Like many popular Web sites, Boing Boing has a long history; it was first launched as a small independent print zine.

their films are not made or are not developed because of a lack of funds. If filmmakers are able to finish their movies, the places where their films can be screened and distributed are limited. These films are usually left in the hands of the big motion-picture companies and multiplex cinemas. Just as writers have turned to blogging to reach the masses, aspiring filmmakers have turned to video blogs, or vlogging, to get their films screened on the Internet. The success of YouTube has turned everybody into a videomaker; some people seek to gain exposure to their videos, while others just look to have fun. Vlog pioneer Adrian Miles, who posted the first-ever vlog (also called vog) entry in 2000, says, "A vog is personal. [It] uses available technology and respects bandwidth. A vog experiments with video and audio. A vog explores the proximate distance of words and moving media."

Because vlogs use available technology and keep files small, they remain manageable for people to view, download, and share.

With vlogs, filmmakers can gain greater exposure to their work in ways that they never imagined before. Consider the success of "It's Jerry Time," a cult vlog that follows the trials of the unfortunate life of Jerry, whose struggles with his animated landlord and equally animated former girlfriend complement his unaffected manner in the face of adversity. "It's Jerry Time" is the creation of Jerry Zucker, who writes the stories, creates the music and voices, and stars in the vlog. Zucker's brother, Orrin, uses a single digital camera and animates the video with the graphics software Adobe After Effects. The success of "It's Jerry Time" includes the sale of a DVD and it was nominated for an Emmy Award in 2006. Because of this achievement, other filmmakers are scrambling to create their own vlogs and to promote them using social networks.

PES is another vlogger who was able to take his skills for creating video and turn them into a viable business. Eatpes.com, home of the twisted films of PES, is an amazing catalog of fantastic short films. Shot in stop-motion animation using ordinary objects, PES turns the everyday into the extraordinary. PES's work, which

he started purely for experimentation and fun, has generated some commercial success.

What all of these former amateur video- and film-makers share is that they each used social networks to help them promote their work.

Actors and performers can benefit from self-promotion via social networking on the Internet, too. Comedian Dane Cook has risen to the summit of stand-up comedy with equal parts of talent and the self-promotion. Cook's rise to fame was supported in part by the investment of his life savings of $25,000 on a content-rich Web site in 2002. Previous comedians had never fully investigated the Web's potential, nor had they set up MySpace pages as Cook had done. He had more than 1.5 million MySpace friends in 2007. He has used his marketing skills and ability to utilize social networking tools to push himself to the top of the stand-up comedy arena.

Chet Zar, a special-effects makeup artist, designer, and sculptor for the film industry, saw his success as a painter skyrocket after he coupled his personal Web page with a profile on MySpace. In Zar's opinion, people no longer need personal Web pages because having a profile on a social network functions in much the same way. His point is that there is already a community associated with MySpace, whereas a Web page has to be searched for in a specific way. In addition, a social network enables you to connect with other artists and musicians and helps to bring more traffic to your profile. Zar includes regular updates as a part of his MySpace profile and links everything back to his

Comedian Dane Cook, who uses social networking to market himself, poses backstage after being a presenter at the sixty-fourth annual Golden Globe Awards in 2007.

Web site, where prints of his works are available for purchase. He believes that MySpace has launched his career as a painter and encourages other artists (especially those without start-up capital) to use social networks to gain much-needed exposure. Zar said, "When you are starting out and have no money and not a lot of product to offer, one thing you can offer fans that doesn't cost anything is personal communication. They really appreciate that, especially in this cold and impersonal corporate culture."

Today, more and more people are advancing their careers and finding increased opportunities by taking advantage of social networking. In the simplest terms, making widespread connections via social networking sites allows you to reach more people more quickly and more often. Artist Carrie Ann Baade senses a shift in the way people will get their work seen and into the public's hands. In a telephone interview in 2006, Baade said, "The tables have turned. Artists used to send their slides to galleries and now they simply send their Web URL. I have had ten times as much response by corresponding through MySpace and e-mail than I ever did [when I took a more] traditional route." Like so many people know, Baade believes that social networks have made the entire world a more intimate place to live and to do business in: "There is the art image, face, and name connection with MySpace." However, Baade does warn of the pitfalls of getting involved in online communities. She recommends being ready to block someone who makes inappropriate comments.

Making Friends and Staying Safe

Here are some helpful guidelines to follow while social networking:

- Never post personal information such as your address, phone number, Social Security number, or location or name of your school on your personal profile.
- Set your profile to "Private" so that only people you know can view it.
- Be sure to read the Privacy Policy carefully before clicking on "I Agree" when you set up any account.
- When interacting with strangers, be careful about the kind of information you reveal to them.
- Make sure you are comfortable sharing with the world the profile, blogs, pictures, etc., that you post. Remember that the information you post is available to anyone and everyone unless you set your profile to "Private."

 You should never offer personal information such as your phone number or address on your MySpace profile. For added protection, many people lie about their location, age, or marital status to deflect unwanted attention.

CHAPTER THREE

EVALUATING YOUR SKILLS

As the Internet has evolved, social networks such as MySpace have created a place where all people who interact on the Web are brought together in one place. These networks have become important elements of people's lives, promoting the concept of community in a sea of digital information. Social networks have not only enhanced the experience of connecting with people, they have also made it easier to promote local events, including concerts, readings, film screenings, shows, and art openings.

Social networking has evolved from being a means for socializing to being a tool for promoting people who may need to further themselves or for

Today, most new computers are set up for video chatting. This teen is using a video camera that is attached to her monitor.

advancing a hobby or skill that they want to turn into a career.

Using Your Digital Skills for Self-Promotion

Social networking has allowed artists, writers, performers, musicians, and filmmakers to connect with one another. These people use social networks to gain exposure for their work and to find opportunities in related industries. For instance, graphic artists use social networks to sell their illustrations, and illustrators are able to find jobs in graphic design and to be in contact with art directors who are in search of new work. Musicians can find work in films by performing musical scores, and composers for film can connect with other musicians to form bands.

 There are countless Web sites devoted to self-promotion, especially in fields that concern the arts, such as film, photography, painting and drawing, and playing music. In fact, MySpace was especially designed to promote unsigned bands and is still largely used for that purpose. Other useful Web sites for self-promotion are PortfolioCity.com, Saatchi-gallery.co.uk (both show student work), and etsy.com (a place to sell your handmade crafts). Musicians who are interested in promotion beyond MySpace can consider PromoteYourBand.co.uk, OurBand.net, BandBuzzer.com, and CDBaby.com (to sell independent music).

The skills that you might use to create a good profile on MySpace or Facebook might be the kinds of skills you could use in a career in the future. Digital skills such as

New computer software programs enable users to draw on screen, but some drawing skills remain more traditional, such as creating animation.

page layout and design, illustration, photography, creating animation, editing video, and composing music may help you decide which career to pursue. These digital skills immediately can be put to use to determine if working in these areas is something you would enjoy. You also can begin thinking about how to refine your digital skills to create a spectacular résumé.

 Among the best ways to showcase your talent is to upload your résumé to your personal Web site. Most newer computer models are installed with tutorial software to create simple pages for the Web. There are also hundreds of Web sites devoted exclusively to that purpose. For starters, visit SitePoint.com, WebSource.net, Build-Your-Website.co.uk, or PersonalWeb.about.com. For tips and tricks for using software such as Adobe PhotoShop, visit Adobe.com, Graphic-Design.com, SketchPad.net, PhotoshopCafe.com, or PhotoshopKillerTips.com.

If you like graphic design and know a little HTML or XML, then try your hand at designing a Web page or a MySpace profile for a local or home-based business. Because you are still learning the ropes, give yourself plenty of time and room for error so that you can learn from your mistakes. Because you are working for experience only (and not financial compensation), much of the pressure is off. Learn how to work with a business owner to understand the ins and outs of his or her business. What are the most important aspects of the site? What is important to show? How can you help viewers get the "feel" of the business or learn about its top products or services? Working on a Web site from scratch will get

you thinking like a designer and asking the questions and solving the problems just as any professional does. If you like design but don't know code, take a class or team up with someone who knows the basics. You might even start a Web design business together!

If you like to write, try starting a blog, or perhaps ask your friends if they need any promotional writing done. You can write a press release about an upcoming event or performance, a news article for your hometown or high school newspaper, or even a one-sheet biography for a friend's garage band. Attend a local college theater or musical event and cover it as a guest journalist. Afterward, try to get your work printed in a local newspaper or newsletter, or publish your work yourself in a blog or e-zine. Once you get the hang of things, organize editorial and design teams. It will be extremely helpful to show that you can manage a detailed task, such as creating a small monthly or quarterly newsletter or e-zine, or updating a regular Web site with both text and images, if and when you complete a college admissions application.

 If you like to draw, make simple animations. You can begin by either shooting a series of photographs or drawing a series of sequential images. Once you have enough images, animate them by learning animation software such as Macromedia's Flash. Then show off your work on sites like Google Video or YouTube. Perhaps you can make additional animation for local businesses or friends who want something more eye-catching on their blogs, eBay pages, or MySpace profiles.

The Funky Flea

As an art collector and enthusiast, I have been able to enhance my own ability to reach out to artists, view their work online, and learn about their upcoming shows and gallery openings by social networking. In this capacity, I have learned a great deal about an artist and his or her work before attending a gallery opening or deciding to invest in a particular piece. Being able to find art that was shown in galleries in parts of the country I couldn't visit or to view work that wasn't being shown at all except within an online community was a revelation. Being able to connect with artists and hear their individual stories only improved my experiences.

Within time, my art collection became impressive enough to share with others, so I decided to host local events to exhibit the work. This opportunity enabled me to ask other artists to participate, including musicians who played live sets and filmmakers who screened their films and videos. Eventually, craftspeople were also taking part, and the event became known as the Funky Flea.

I wanted to share these multimedia experiences with as many people as I could, so I used social networks to reach out to those people within a fifty-mile radius of my home. It was equivalent to handing out fliers in 100 different places simultaneously, and the results were overwhelmingly positive. Now when the Funky Flea is held, my community's small downtown is transformed into an arts festival. The celebration spills out into the streets until the whole town comes alive.

If you are someone who is accomplished in using audio or video processing and editing software, creating videos for YouTube, or making mix CDs for parties, you might have a future in the film or music industry. Take existing video footage you've shot and create a story around the footage of video by editing them together. Or take news clips from television and create a "documentary" by cutting in footage of interviews with people about those news items. You can take existing video and replace the music or dialogue with your own, creating a spoof of the original.

QUICK TIP

Sony Vegas Digital Video and Audio software (for PCs) is a great beginner program for editing video and music together.

You might want to take existing songs and remix them. Splice sections of your favorite songs together to make new songs. You also can find loop and sample CDs at most music stores, which contain license-free audio bytes of music. Software such as Acid will let you build songs from drum, guitar, orchestral, and sound effects loop CDs to create your own music. Once you've finished your video or music projects, put them up on MySpace or YouTube, and let people enjoy them.

If you are someone who is naturally social and always seems to know about every secret party, or your peers are always inviting you to social events, perhaps you can make a future for yourself in public relations (PR) or advertising. Try your hand at organizing or promoting a charity event for your school, such as to raise money for a

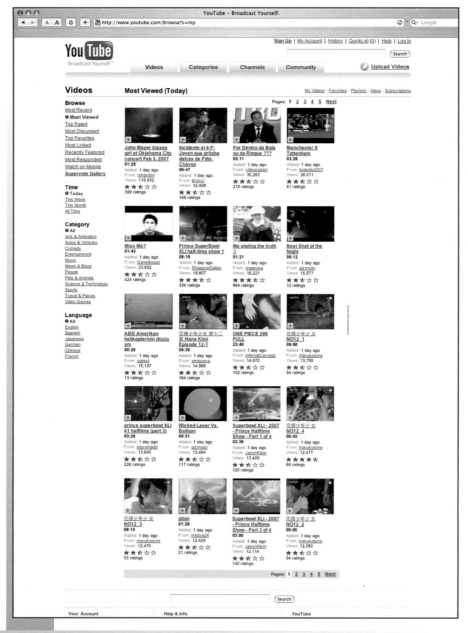

YouTube (YouTube.com), a Web site where anyone can upload personal videos, has virtually transformed the way people use the Internet for entertainment. Every year, fewer people are getting their entertainment from television.

school band trip. What are some of the creative ways that you can think of to get the word out about the event? How much time do you have? What sort of fund-raiser would be a huge hit? Get together with your friends and take a vote. As the PR director, you have to set a date, get the word out, estimate your needs, write a press release, and bring everyone together for a common goal. A successful fund-raiser will often lead to more events on your schedule. If you liked being the person in charge, and the ability of getting everything together comes naturally to you, consider organizing a series social events gatherings such as parties. Learning how to plan charity events and other gatherings on a large scale demonstrates a variety of skills that are great to list on a college application.

If you enjoy taking pictures, go on assignment and photograph interesting subjects. Group some similar images on a photo-sharing site like Flickr or Shutterfly, and then think about starting a blog that features your best work. With your blog as your "calling card," you might be able to supply images for local newspapers, newsletters, or even magazines.

As you increase your skills, you can incorporate the use of social networks to increase your overall exposure, attendance, feedback, and the potential for future opportunities. If you have the drive to follow a project through to the very end, and you are navigating through the hills and valleys of the Internet, you'll ultimately find the career you're seeking. Keep the following in mind: when you are using social networking sites to spread the message about your accomplishments, paint in broad strokes and fill in the details later. What this

Bake sales are no longer limited to having only a few customers. Social networking sites can inform people of community events and happenings to ensure larger turnouts.

means is that you should examine your talents truthfully and then concentrate on your most important and relevant skills. You can almost think of your profile page as your résumé. As you gain new skills or broaden your existing goals, you can always update it. Keeping your profile fresh is important, especially when sending new people to view your information.

CHAPTER FOUR

SHAPING YOUR GOALS

The digital world offers young people more ways to learn skills that may be valuable for future careers. These careers include writing, taking photographs, creating dynamic graphic designs, and marketing using any number of methods, including video and audio recordings. Social networking sites help make these careers possible. MySpace, for example, is a great place not only for artists to connect with magazines or galleries, but also for musicians to be introduced to bands and record labels. MySpace also employs dozens of artists who are responsible for the look and feel of the site.

Social networks organize the world so that finding your market, whether you are an artist, an entrepreneur,

Graphic designers usually work in teams when building fresh Web pages or rebuilding existing ones.

MySpace (MySpace.com) is unique as a social network because of the elaborate matrix that is created as users increase their number of contacts, also known as "friends."

or both, and interacting with that market are as simple as a couple of clicks on the mouse. The best social networks are full of tools that are easy to find and use, and have search capabilities powerful and flexible enough to find exactly who you're looking for. Tools such as e-mail, groups, bulletins, and comments can help you express who you are and what you have to offer. Profile searches with geographic, age, and interest filters help narrow down exactly who gets your information. Being able to find your target market not only gives you contacts that are useful, it also shows potential employers that you have initiative. This proactive means of marketing might lead you to experiences that will bolster your college application and job résumé. You could even be on the road to a self-made career.

To get the ball rolling, you'll need to go on a little fact-finding mission so that you can realize your vision. You need to define your goals, identify and evaluate your skills, determine what connections need to be made and how to make them, and organize and present your work so that your best talents shine through.

Assess Your Skills

Identifying and evaluating your skills are essential steps in determining a career path. Once you've assessed your qualifications, you can research what sorts of careers best match your skills. For example, you might like shooting footage with your digital video camera, using it to create movies. What part of the process of making a movie do you enjoy the most? Maybe it's the editing aspect that keeps you excited about the project, cutting sections of video together to give it a narrative shape or to create a specific look and feel. You may decide to get into the film industry as an editor. Or maybe you're a writer whose work is very visual or someone who sees his or her stories in pictures. If this is the case, you may decide that writing or illustrating children's books or graphic novels and comics would be a good fit. Or writing copy or slogans for advertising agencies may offer you a nice way of making a living while still giving you a way to express your creative side. The idea is that the more knowledgeable you are

Who Should I Contact?

Sometimes a concept is easier to understand when you can see it in pictures, graphs, charts, or tables. Here is a list of potential areas of interests and those who make a living in those areas:

- **Art**: Illustrators, gallery owners, critics, art directors, stock illustration houses, advertising directors, children's book authors, graphic designers, Web designers, and art collectors.
- **Music**: Composers, performers, photographers, critics, producers, magazine and newspaper editors, nightclub and bar owners, producers, record labels, record company executives, public relations professionals, consumers, and tech gurus.
- **Film**: Camera operators and tech crews, film and video editors, sound engineers, movie directors, producers, talent scouts, screenwriters, actors, art house theaters, consumers, animators, special effects artists, set designers, performers, musicians, puppeteers, and visual artists.
- **Writing**: Screenwriters, playwrights, poets, book editors, newspaper editors, magazine editors, publishers, illustrators, professional organizations of writers and illustrators, art directors, agents, acquisition editors, copyeditors and proofreaders, bloggers, authors' agencies, and photographers.
- **Performance**: Singers, vocal coaches, actors, dancers, comedians, screenwriters, musicians, filmmakers, videographers, documentarians, journalists, and photographers.

about your skills, the easier it will be to decide what careers might be good for you.

Look for Mentors

For inspiration, find people who have had success in the fields that interest you. Explore and research what it is that helped make them successful. Having a better idea of what they did to reach their level of achievement should go a long way in showing you what you will need to do to be successful. The people whom you will need to know will be your connections to help bridge the gap between who you are and what you want to be. It's important to realize who these people are and how to track them down, and once you have, what to show and tell them.

 If you're a musician who wants to sell your music, seek out bands and other musicians who were able to become top-selling artists by using the "word-of-mouth" power of the social networks. What is it about their story that is different from little-known bands that you can extract and use to your benefit? What did they do right that most everyone else did wrong?

One thing that you will discover is that a successful artist has to find out who his or her audience is. Having done that, he or she needs to discern where that audience is hiding. Once you know where those people are and how they can be reached, what you show and tell them will have to have an impact. Remember that you get only one chance to make a first impression.

Success Stories

Brad Ogden, a seventeen-year-old high school junior, logged so many hours putting together his Sterling Heights, Michigan, Web page design company that his girlfriend broke up with him, even though he earned $540,000 in 2005, according to YoungBiz.com. Ogden got into Web page design when he was just thirteen years old, creating a company he called Virtual Web Pages.

In 2003, when Michael Furdyk launched a help line from his family's basement in a Toronto, Canada, suburb to explain how the Internet works, it was done just for fun. A chat room fan, Furdyk became pals with sixteen-year-old Michael Hayman, who was living in Australia. The two like-minded teens decided to become business partners in 1997 and to run MyDesktop.com, a help site that Hayman had already launched in Australia. At first, the site focused on helping people with Windows problems. Later, it expanded to include information on games and other topics, widening the customer base and making them very successful. Today, Furdyk helps to manage a new Web site, a social network for students called TakingITGlobal.org. He cofounded the network to help connect young people with various social causes. He and his network of more than 130,000 students are helping to make a difference in their communities.

Angelo Sotira's obsession with his music Web site led him from Poughkeepsie, New York, to Hollywood, California, right after his high school graduation in 2004. Sotira works exclusively with Hollywood power broker Michael Ovitz. Ovitz, head of Artists Management Group,

 Michael Furdyk, cofounder of TakingITGlobal.org, has been involved in Internet community building and social networking since the late 1990s. TakingITGlobal has connected thousands of teens who want to change the world for the better.

bought Sotira's Web site in 2005 through his investment company, Lynx Technology Group. Today, Sotira works out of Ovitz's Wilshire Boulevard offices as the CEO of Dimension Music, a music portal with online disk jockeys.

Sixteen-year-old Ava Lowery takes politicians' quotes and creates animations with video clips and music for her Web site, PeaceTakesCourage.com. She was profiled on CNN and *Larry King Live* in December 2006, and was the toast of the 2006 Daily KOS Convention, an annual get-together of liberal bloggers.

CHAPTER FIVE

GETTING THE WORD OUT

Your profile in a social network is the way the rest of the community will see you. Because your profile becomes their perception of you, it should be organized so that its images and content portray the real you.

If you are a visual artist, like a graphic designer, animator, painter, or filmmaker, you will want your profile to reflect these creative pursuits. Include images and video clips of your work in a way that sets you apart from other visual artists. If you are a musician, you will want to incorporate audio clips of your music and live and studio images of the band members. You might also want to include images of your album covers or sample lyrics so

In addition to regular curricula, many schools provide programs that teach technology and Web site creation skills to students.

Next time you go on a trip, bring your camera. Increasingly, professional publications are relying on talented amateurs to provide them with unique images, including underwater photographs.

that your audience has an increased understanding of who you are and what you are expressing.

If you are a writer, your profile should include a sample chapter from your work or an article or other written text. In each case, your profile should represent who you are and should be a dynamic, ever-evolving peek into your creative personality.

If you organize your page effectively, not only will people see your work for what it is, but they also will see that you thoughtfully have expressed your ideas about how best to represent yourself.

Finding Contacts

Social networks have a multitude of tools that make defining your vision easy, including methods to display and keep track of the connections you've made. Just getting involved in an online community will expose you to a massive group of people who share common interests and philosophies. Just monitoring the activities in an online community can give you an idea of the potential of social networking. For instance, when I first started using MySpace, I wanted my profile to be a place where artists would come and post comments about their upcoming shows. Comments are public postings that you can add to someone else's profile page for the rest of the people who visit that person's page to see. As an art collector, this was an effective way to get updates of art shows and available works for purchase. I also liked the idea of helping artists by giving them another place to promote their work. Adding artists as

Be Your Own Archivist

Selling who you are is sometimes as important as selling your skills or your work. Even though not everything an artist makes should become part of his or her professional portfolio, everything an artist creates should be preserved. Act as your own archivist. Your history as an artist will be a big part of your success. Your volume of work, including unfinished writings, works in progress, behind-the-scenes footage, deleted scenes, demo tapes, and half-finished paintings, make up the history of your achievements. The story behind any business or artistic venture is a major part of the appeal of the work or the business itself. It's the story that's often featured in press releases and articles, and it's a pivotal piece of the puzzle that makes up your individual story. Archive all your work: the scribbles and doodles, the rants in a crumpled notebook, the out-of-focus photos, or the video captures too unpolished to finish. It's all this work that shows where you come from, and it explains who you are today.

contacts (or, as MySpace calls them, "friends") allows you access to their profiles, where you can place comments, but also includes them as recipients to any bulletins that you might post.

If you have a skill that you are trying to promote, you can start spreading the word by searching for people in the community who would be important connections in your quest for success. Communicate with them one on one, exchange ideas, and seek advice. You can communicate your thoughts in bulletins or blogs or by sending a mass e-mail to all your contacts at one time. This is how I first reached out to artists to advertise on my MySpace profile. The more contacts I created, the more visibility my profile page received. Words spread virally on the Internet in an exponential fashion. You tell two friends, and they tell two friends, and so on. It isn't long before you've built up a treasure chest of connections. As that list grows, the number of people you can get your message out to through comments, bulletins, blogs, and event listings grows along with it.

Your friends also have friends with whom you might like to connect, increasing your contact list further. Check through your friends' contact lists and see whom you'd like to meet. When you find someone you'd like to have as a contact, make sure you send a personal message to him or her before you request to be added to their "friends" list. Tell the person why you'd like to be added to his or her contact list. Personal messages are still the best way to communicate with people.

The whole idea about social networking and being part of a community is treating people the way you'd want to be treated. If you allow people to post comments on your profile page, they'll be more willing to let you post on their pages. Every comment you post is like a large billboard for the rest of the community to see. The more you can post your message on other people's pages, the more that message will be seen.

Once people start to see your comments on other people's pages, you'll start to get requests to be added as

When checking out social networks to advertise your skills, don't overlook the many job placement and career-building Web sites that are available, such as CareerBuilder (CareerBuilder.com), Monster, HotJobs, and Indeed.

a contact on your profile page. Having your contact list grow on its own will help increase the number of your contacts.

Groups and forums are great ways to convey your message. Find ones that are relevant to helping you achieve your career goals. Examine the lists of topics discussed and get involved in some of the discussions that might be of particular interest to you. Start your own topics by seeking out advice from other participants. You can also search the member lists of these groups and forums to find new contacts.

Above all, remember that reaching your career goals takes time and persistence. It may mean that you have to refine your work through trial and error. Fortunately, creating a digital representation of yourself and your work will allow you to constantly update your profile, improve your skills, and let your talents shine.

GLOSSARY

archivist Someone who is responsible for compiling a person's total works, usually chronologically.

avatar An electronic visual representation of oneself or someone else.

blog A Web log, diary, or journal; a Web page where content is added regularly.

HTML Acronym that stands for hypertext markup language, a programming language that is used for creating Web pages.

hyperlink A word or string of words in an electronic document that links those words to a related electronic document, often a Web page.

portfolio A body of professional work, such as a group of paintings, drawings, photographs, videos, films, etc.

profile A personal page on a social network that is visible to other members of that network. A profile often contains text, images, audio and video files, and contact information.

six degrees of separation A theory that all human beings are connected through relationships with, at most, six other people.

social network An electronic "community" of people who are represented by information they add to profiles and who can communicate with one another by using a variety of methods.

URL Acronym that stands for uniform resource locator, the address of a Web page, often starting with www (for World Wide Web).

vlog Literally, a video log; similar to a blog (or Web log).

XML Acronym that stands for extensible markup language, a programming language becoming popular for the Web.

FOR MORE INFORMATION

Blog Safety
http://www.blogSafety.com

Connect for Kids
http://www.connectforkids.org

Social Software Weblog
http://socialsoftware.weblogsinc.com/2005/02/14/
  home-of-the-social-networking-services-meta-list

WiredSafety.org
http://www.wiredsafety.org

Web Sites

Due to the changing nature of Internet links, Rosen
Publishing has developed an online list of Web sites
related to the subject of this book. This site is updated
regularly. Please use this link to access the list:

http://www.rosenlinks.com/dcb/cbsn

FOR FURTHER READING

Aker, Bob. *Guerrilla Music Marketing Handbook: 201 Self-Promotion Ideas for Songwriters, Musicians, and Bands.* St. Louis, MO: Spotlight Publications, 2001.

Baker, Bob. *MySpace Music Marketing: How to Promote and Sell Your Music on the World's Biggest Networking Site.* St. Louis, MO: Music Marketing Books, 2006.

Buckley, Peter. *The Rough Guide to MySpace & Online Communities.* New York, NY: Penguin Putnam, 2007.

Jenkins, Henry. "Confronting the Challenges of Participatory Culture: Media Education for the 21st Century." The John D. and Catherine T. MacArthur Foundation. 2006. Retrieved January 24, 2007 (http://www.macfound.org/site/c.lkLXJ8MQKrH/b.1038727/apps/s/content.asp?ct=2946895).

Magid, Larry, and Anne Collier. *MySpace Unraveled: What It Is and How to Use It Safely.* Berkeley, CA: Peach Pit Press, 2006.

Manas, Steve. *Your Space: A Friend's Guide to MySpace.* Charleston, SC: BookSurge Publishing, 2006.

BIBLIOGRAPHY

Baade, Carrie Ann. Online interview with the author. November 15, 2006.

BBCNews. "Social Networks Top Google Search." Retrieved November 28, 2006 (http://news.bbc.co.uk/1/hi/technology/6189809.stm).

"The Face of Facebook." Hotseat column, *Wired* magazine, December 2006.

Hansell, Saul. "Technology: Joining the Party, Eager to Make Friends." *New York Times*, October 16, 2006. Retrieved November 28, 2006 (http://select.nytimes.com/search/restricted/article?res=F00F12F83A5B0C748CDDA80994DE404482).

Ives, Nat. "The Media Business: Advertising; A New Type of Pitch to the Online Crowd Mixes Pop Stars and Personals." *New York Times*, December 3, 2004. Retrieved November 28, 2006 (http://select.nytimes.com/search/restricted/article?res=F10D10F6345A0C708CDDAB0994DC404482).

Levine, Robert. "MySpace Aims for Global Audience, and Finds Some Stiff Competition." *New York Times*, November 7, 2006. Retrieved November 28, 2006 (http://select.nytimes.com/search/restricted/article?res=F00F12F83A5B0C748CDDA80994DE404482).

Rivlin, Gary. "Friendster, Love, and Money; Users Lose the Thrill of 'Social Networking.'" *New York Times*, January 24, 2005. Retrieved November 28, 2006 (http://select.nytimes.com/search/restricted/article?res=F20F14F8355C0C778EDDA80894DD404482).

Yang, Jonathan. *The Rough Guide to Blogging*. New York,
NY: Penguin Putnam, 2006.

Zar, Chet. Online interview with the author.
November 19, 2006.

Zucker, Jerry. Online interview with the author.
November 21, 2006.

INDEX

About the Author

Alex Goetchius has written a collection of short stories entitled *Lost in Asbury Park* (2007). He is a cofounder of Curious Interactive, creators of the innovative online arts and culture community Glubdub.com. Glubdub is an online magazine whose content is created by its community. (It's where creative minds come to play.)

Photo Credits

Cover, p. 1, © www.istockphoto.com; p. 27 © Getty Images; pp. 4, 30, 50 © Shutterstock; p. 32 © Spencer Grant/ Photo Edit; pp. 39, 41 © Michael Newmnan/Photo Edit; p. 47 © The Lavin Agency; p. 49 © Peter Byron/Photo Edit.

Designer: Nelson Sá
Photo Researcher: Marty Levick